DINOSAURS!

VELOCIRAPTOR
AND OTHER RAPTORS AND
SMALL CARNIVORES

by
David West

Gareth Stevens
Publishing

Please visit our Web site, www.garethstevens.com.
For a free color catalog of all our high-quality books,
call toll free 1-800-542-2595 or fax 1-877-542-2596.

Library of Congress Cataloging-in-Publication Data

West, David, 1956-
Velociraptor and other raptors and small carnivores / David West.
p. cm. — (Dinosaurs!)
Includes index.
ISBN 978-1-4339-4225-9 (pbk.)
ISBN 978-1-4339-4226-6 (6 pack)
ISBN 978-1-4339-4224-2 (lib. bdg.)
1. Velociraptor—Juvenile literature. 2. Carnivora, Fossil—Juvenile literature. I. Title.
QE862.S3W469 2011
567.912—dc22

2010015867

First Edition

Published in 2011 by
Gareth Stevens Publishing
111 East 14th Street, Suite 349
New York, NY 10003

Copyright © 2011 David West Books

Designed by David West Books
Editor: Ronne Randall

Printed in China

CPSIA compliance information: Batch #DS10GS: For further information contact Gareth Stevens, New York, New York at 1-800-542-2595.

Contents

What Are Raptors and Small **Carnivores**?

Many of the dinosaurs in this book belong to the group of **theropod** dinosaurs called maniraptora. They are closely related to birds and include dromaeosaurids (raptors), **troodontids**, **therizinosaurids**, **oviraptorids**, and early birds. Also included are other types of small meat-eating theropods that lived alongside the giant carnivores.

Dinosaurs lived throughout the Mesozoic Era, which is divided into three periods, shown here. It is sometimes called the Age of the Reptiles. Dinosaurs first appeared in the Upper Triassic period and died out during a ***mass extinction event*** *65 million years ago.*

BRAINS

Most of these dinosaurs had big brains for their size. This suggests they were quite intelligent compared with other dinosaurs.

EYESIGHT

These **predators** had good eyesight. Some had eyes that faced slightly forward, giving the animals **binocular** vision.

SERRATED TEETH

Many of these predators had sharp, **serrated** teeth. These were ideal for slicing through the flesh of prey.

Deinonychus

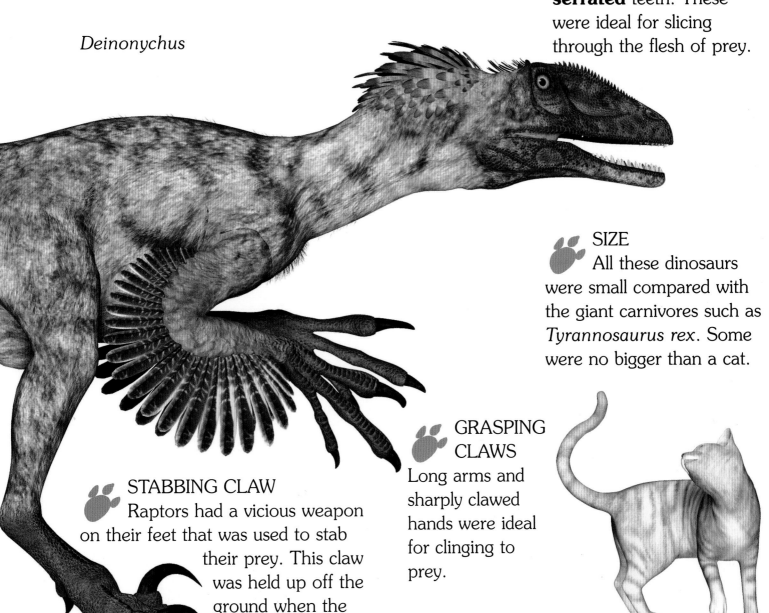

SIZE

All these dinosaurs were small compared with the giant carnivores such as *Tyrannosaurus rex*. Some were no bigger than a cat.

STABBING CLAW

Raptors had a vicious weapon on their feet that was used to stab their prey. This claw was held up off the ground when the raptor ran.

GRASPING CLAWS

Long arms and sharply clawed hands were ideal for clinging to prey.

227	205	180	159	144	98	65 Millions of years ago (mya)
Upper	Lower	Middle	Upper	Lower	Upper	
TRIASSIC		JURASSIC		CRETACEOUS		

Upper Cretaceous
70 mya
Argentina

Austroraptor

Austroraptor, meaning "southern thief," is among the largest of the raptors found to date. It belonged to the dromaeosaurids, or birdlike dinosaurs that walked on two legs, the most famous of which was *Velociraptor*.

Austroraptor differed from other raptors not just in size. It had a long head and conical teeth similar to spinosaurs. It had short arms and stout legs, which is also unusual for a raptor. Scientists believe it was a fierce fighting animal, in a league with larger dinosaurs such as

A group of hungry Austroraptors *close in on a dying* Argyrosaurus, *a **titanosaur**, in this scene from Upper Cretaceous South America. Normally, a titanosaur would be too big for these raptors to tackle.*

Tyrannosaurus rex. It has been suggested that *Austroraptor,* like other raptors, had feathers. It would have used its powerful long jaws, lined with pointed teeth, to grab hold of its prey. A large claw on each foot was used like a dagger to stab its victim. These fierce creatures would have been a terrifying sight to all but the largest of dinosaurs.

Austroraptor was about 16 feet (4.9 m) long and weighed around 810 pounds (368 kg).

7

Coelophysis

Coelophysis, meaning "hollow form," was named for its hollow arm and leg bones. It was a slim, lightly built theropod that was one of the early dinosaurs. It was a very fast runner, which helped it chase down its prey.

Coelophysis had large eyes and good eyesight. Its neck and head were long, as was its tail, which may have acted as a counterweight to balance the animal when it turned at high speeds. Its long, narrow head had jaws filled with sharp, curved, serrated teeth. This suggests

A pack of Coelophysises *chase after small lizards along a dry riverbed in this scene from Upper Triassic North America. Fossils of many* Coelophysises *have been found together, suggesting that these dinosaurs may have lived in groups.*

that it was a meat eater preying on small, lizardlike animals. It may also have hunted in packs to tackle larger prey. It seems that *Coelophysis* may have lived beside streams, and fish may have been part of its diet. The many *Coelophysis* fossils that have been found together were probably the result of a flash flood that swept away a large number of *Coelophysises* and buried them quickly.

Coelophysis grew up to 9.8 feet (3 m) long and weighed around 55 pounds (25 kg).

Compsognathus

Compsognathus, meaning "dainty jaw," was a small, carnivorous theropod. Its delicate skull was narrow and long, with a thin snout. The eyes were large in proportion to the rest of the skull. Its teeth were small but sharp, suited for a diet of small lizards and insects.

Compsognathus was a small, two-legged dinosaur with long legs and a very long tail, which it used for balance. Its arms were smaller than its legs and had three fingers ending with claws suited for grasping prey.

A large group of Compsognathuses *disturb a flock of* Rhamphorhynchuses *that have gathered to feed off the carcass of a dead* **plesiosaur**. *Living at the same time as* Compsognathus *were the* **pterosaur** Pterodactylus *and the early bird* Archaeopteryx.

Compsognathus lived in Europe, which was, during the Upper Jurassic, a dry, tropical **archipelago** at the edge of the Tethys Sea. There were **lagoons** situated between the beaches and coral reefs of these Jurassic European islands. No other dinosaur has been found with *Compsognathus*, indicating that this little theropod might have been the main land predator of these islands.

Compsognathus grew up to 2.3 feet (0.7 m) long and weighed between 1.8 and 7.7 pounds (0.82 and 3.5 kg).

Deinonychus

Deinonychus, which means "terrible claw," was a dromaeosaurid. This small, sleek dinosaur with a huge sickle-like claw on each foot was an active and very fast predator.

Although feathers have not been found with fossils of Deinonychus, evidence suggests that dromaeosaurids, including Deinonychus, had feathers. Fossils of earlier and later dromaeosaurids that were closely related to Deinonychus have been found with feather markings.

A *pack of* Deinonychuses *brings down a young* Tenontosaurus *while others chase off an adult in this scene from Lower Cretaceous North America.* Deinonychus *fossil remains have been found with those of the ornithopod* Tenontosaurus.

Geological evidence suggests that *Deinonychus* lived in a floodplain or swamplike habitat. It may have hunted in packs, attacking its prey by using its large claws to stab and slash while it held on with its clawed fingers. When running, the dinosaur held its large claws up off the ground. Its brain was large for a dinosaur, so it was probably fairly intelligent.

Deinonychus grew up to 9.8 feet (3 m) long and weighed up to 130 pounds (59 kg)

Gallimimus

Gallimimus, meaning "chicken mimic," was an **ornithomimosaur** (bird-mimic lizard) that resembled an ostrich. Like a bird, it was feathered (though its feathers were short), and like an ostrich, it could run very fast. It was probably an **omnivore**.

Gallimimus had three clawed fingers on each hand and long legs with three clawed toes on each foot. A long tail acted as a counterbalance and stabilizer during fast turns while running after prey or away from

14

The Gallimimus *in this scene from Upper Cretaceous Asia has been caught stealing eggs from the nest of a* Tarbosaurus. *However, it should be swift enough to outrun the giant meat-eating theropod.*

predators. Its bones were hollow like those of modern birds, which saved weight and helped it run faster. *Gallimimus* probably fed on lizards, eggs, and insects. Its long, toothless snout ended in a beak that would have been useful for cracking open dinosaur eggs. *Gallimimus* was present in large numbers during the Upper Cretaceous period and may have lived in herds.

Gallimimus grew up to 19.7 feet (6 m) long and weighed little more than 440 pounds (200 kg).

15

Gigantoraptor

Gigantoraptor, meaning "giant thief," belonged to the same family as *Oviraptor* (see pp. 20–21). However, *Gigantoraptor* was much larger than other members of the family. Its discovery stunned experts. No one had expected birdlike dinosaurs to be so big.

Although *Gigantoraptor* could not fly, it was covered in feathers and had short arms ending in large, clawed hands. It had a long, ostrichlike neck and a head that resembled a bird's, with a powerful snapping

A pair of Gigantoraptors *chase a family of* Protoceratops *in this scene from Upper Cretaceous Asia.* Gigantoraptor's *size and build suggest that it could outrun its prey over long distances.*

beak instead of a toothed jaw. Experts had believed that carnivorous dinosaurs became smaller as they grew more birdlike. But *Gigantoraptor*, which **evolved** near the end of the reign of the dinosaurs, proved that this was not always the case. Detailed study of the fossilized bone structure suggests that this dinosaur had a very fast growth rate, which may explain its size.

Gigantoraptor grew to 26.2 feet (8 m) long and weighed about 1.5 tons (1.4 metric tons).

Microraptor

Microraptor means "little thief." Like *Archaeopteryx*, this tiny dinosaur provides important evidence of the close link between dinosaurs and birds. *Microraptor* had long flight feathers that formed winglike surfaces on its arms, tail, and also, surprisingly, on its legs.

Microraptor has been described as a four-winged dinosaur, and experts think it may have glided from branch to branch using its feathered arms and legs. Its body had a thick covering of feathers, with a

18

On a rare trip down to the ground, a pair of Microraptors *feed on insects while a third climbs back up a tree for safety. A fourth Microraptor glides to the ground in this scene from Lower Cretaceous Asia.*

diamond-shaped fan at the end of the tail. This was possibly used to steer it during gliding. *Microraptor* probably spent most of its life in trees because the hind wing feathers attached to its feet would have made running on the ground difficult. Its clawed hands and feet were well suited for climbing tree trunks and branches.

Microraptor was about 2.6 feet (0.8 m) long and weighed around 2.2 pounds (1 kg).

Oviraptor

Oviraptor means "egg thief." It was given the name because an *Oviraptor* fossil was found on top of some eggs, and people assumed that it had been eating them. However, it turns out that it was a parent of the eggs in the nest, so it was not an egg stealer but a **nurturer**.

Oviraptor is a member of a specialized group of theropods called oviraptorosaurai. It was lightly built, fast moving, and long legged. Its body was covered in feathers that might have been brightly colored in

20

In the early morning sunshine, a male Oviraptor *dances and shows off his colorful feathers. Three female* Oviraptors *watch his* **courtship** *display as a pair of* Bactrosauruses *walk past in this scene from Upper Cretaceous Mongolia.*

the male. It had a long tail with a fan of feathers at the end, strong arms, and curved claws on its three-fingered hands and three-toed feet. Its strangely shaped, parrotlike head had a short, toothless beak and extremely powerful jaws. *Oviraptor* had a small, hornlike crest on its head, which was probably used for courtship displays. Fossilized remains of a lizard in its stomach indicate that it ate meat.

Oviraptor was about 7 feet (2.1 m) long and weighed up to 55 pounds (25 kg).

21

Therizinosaurus

Therizinosaurus, "scythe lizard," was a very large, strange-looking member of the maniraptor group. It had a potbelly and giant claws up to 3.3 feet (1 m) long. It was too bulky to run fast enough to catch prey, so experts think it was a plant eater.

The giant claws on each hand would have made terrifying-looking weapons in defense against any predator. Although the claws would have been too heavy to make quick swipes, their size when displayed

A group of Therizinosauruses *with a **juvenile** have an easy time breaking into giant termite mounds to feed on the tiny insects in this scene from Upper Cretaceous Asia. A small group of* Velociraptors *arrive to feed on the leftovers.*

on outstretched arms would have been enough to frighten away the fiercest of predators. The claws were probably used during feeding every day, to drag overhead branches down toward its mouth. Some scientists think that *Therizinosaurus* also used its huge claws to break open giant termite mounds so it could eat the termites.

Therizinosaurus was about 26 feet (8 m) long and weighed up to 4 tons (3.6 metric tons).

23

Troodon

Troodon, which means "wounding tooth," was named
for its strangely serrated teeth, which are different from
the teeth of most other theropods. Experts think it may
have been an omnivore, eating plants as well as
hunting for small prey such as lizards.

Troodon had very long, slender legs, suggesting that it was a fast
runner. It had long arms that folded against its sides, similar to the way
a bird at rest folds its wings. It had large, sickle-shaped claws on its

24

In a forest of pine trees, a male Troodon sits on his nest **brooding**. His female partner has returned from hunting and offers him a lizard she has caught in this scene from Upper Cretaceous North America.

second toes, like a dromaeosaurid. Its eyes were large, which may suggest nighttime activity. The eyes were also slightly forward facing, which gave *Troodon* binocular vision. *Troodon* had one of the largest brains for its size of any dinosaur. Based on fossil evidence, experts think that once the female had laid her eggs, it was the male that sat on the nest and kept them warm.

Troodon grew up to 6.6 feet (2 m) long and weighed around 110 pounds (50 kg).

25

Lower Cretaceous
112–100 mya
United States

Utahraptor

Utahraptor, which means "Utah's predator," got its name because its fossil remains were found in Utah. It is a dromaeosaurid, in the same group as *Deinonychus,* but it is more than double the size of its close cousin. At almost 20 feet (6m) long, it is the largest of all dromaeosaurs.

Like other dromaeosaurids, *Utahraptor* had a huge, curved claw on the second toe of each foot. At 9.4 inches (24 cm) in length, these weapons, along with its clawed grasping hands and razor-sharp teeth,

A *pack of* Utahraptors *hunt down a lone juvenile* Cedarosaurus, *a **brachiosaurid sauropod**, in this scene from Lower Cretaceous North America. Fossil evidence of the closely related* Deinonychus *suggests that* Utahraptors *hunted in packs.*

would have made it a powerful predator. Its toe joints were enlarged so that its weapon claw could be raised upward and backward to avoid damage while running. But when it attacked, its claw flexed forward like a **switchblade**. When hunting in packs, *Utahraptors* could kill prey much larger than themselves, such as the sauropod *Cedarosaurus*.

Utahraptor grew to about 19.7 feet (6 m) long and weighed up to 1,540 pounds (700 kg).

Velociraptor

Velociraptor, meaning "speedy thief," is probably the best-known dromaeosaurid. It was a bipedal, feathered carnivore with a long, stiff tail. Each foot had an enlarged sickle-shaped claw, which is thought to have been used to kill its prey.

Velociraptor can be recognized by its long skull and upturned snout. The jaws were lined on each side with 26 to 28 widely spaced teeth, each more strongly serrated on the back edge than on the front. Teeth

A pack of *Velociraptors run through a sun-dappled forest in Upper Cretaceous Asia. The pack is on the trail of* Protoceratops *(see pp. 16–17). Fossil evidence from Mongolia has revealed a* Velociraptor *in a death struggle with a* Protoceratops.

like these would have improved its ability to catch and hold fast-moving prey. *Velociraptor* had large hands, each with three curved claws. Hunting in packs, these small predators would have been able to kill larger prey such as *Protoceratops*. Experts discovered evidence of feathers on a well-preserved *Velociraptor* forearm, suggesting that they were probably covered in feathers.

Velociraptor grew up to 5.9 feet (1.8 m) long and weighed up to 33 pounds (15 kg).

Animal Gallery

Other dinosaurs and animals that appear in the scenes.

Protoceratops
(pp. 16–17)
"first horned face"
protoceratopsid
Upper Cretaceous
Mongolia, China

Argyrosaurus (pp. 6–7)
"silver lizard"
titanosaur
Upper Cretaceous
Argentina

Rhamphorhynchus
(pp. 10–11)
"beak snout"
pterosaur
Upper Jurassic
Germany, England,
Tanzania, Spain

Tarbosaurus (pp. 14–15)
"alarming lizard"
tyrannosaurid
Upper Cretaceous
Mongolia, China

Tenontosaurus (pp. 12–13)
"sinew lizard"
iguanodont
Lower Cretaceous
Canada, United States

plesiosaur (pp. 10–11)
carnivorous aquatic
reptile
Lower Jurassic to
Upper Cretaceous

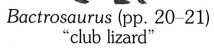

Bactrosaurus (pp. 20–21)
"club lizard"
hadrosaur (duck-billed dinosaur)
Upper Cretaceous
Mongolia

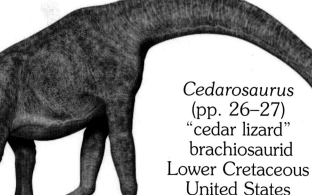

Cedarosaurus
(pp. 26–27)
"cedar lizard"
brachiosaurid
Lower Cretaceous
United States

Glossary

archipelago A chain or group of islands.

binocular Using both eyes to look at an object, which gives good sense of depth.

brachiosaurid A member of the family of plant-eating, four-legged dinosaurs with longer forelegs than hind legs.

brooding Sitting on eggs to hatch them.

carnivores Meat-eating animals.

counterweight A weight that balances a body to keep it level.

courtship Mate-selection rituals.

dromaeosaurid A member of a group of carnivorous dinosaurs known as raptors, with slashing claws on their feet.

evolved Gradually changed by natural selection over a long period of time.

fossils The remains of living things that have turned to rock.

hadrosaur A member of the family of duck-billed dinosaurs.

iguanodont A member of the group of plant-eating dinosaurs that includes *Iguanodon*.

juvenile A youngster.

lagoon A shallow saltwater lake separated from the sea by a sandbank.

mass extinction event A large-scale disappearance of species of animals and plants in a relatively short period of time.

nurturer An animal that looks after and protects its young.

omnivore An animal that eats both plants and meat.

ornithomimosaur Theropod dinosaur that slightly resembled modern ostriches.

oviraptorid A member of the family of birdlike maniraptor dinosaurs.

plesiosaur A type of carnivorous marine reptile that lived during the Age of the Dinosaurs.

predators Animals that hunt and kill other animals for food.

protoceratopsid A member of a family of early beaked dinosaurs.

pterosaur A member of a group of flying reptiles that lived during the Age of the Dinosaurs.

sauropod A member of a group of large plant-eating dinosaurs that had very long necks.

serrated Having a row of sharp points along an edge.

switchblade A knife with a blade that springs open.

therizinosaurid A member of the family of omnivorous theropod dinosaurs with large finger claws.

theropod A member of a two-legged dinosaur family that includes most of the giant carnivorous dinosaurs.

titanosaur A member of a group of very large sauropods.

troodontid A member of a group of small to medium-sized theropods with unusually long legs compared with other theropods and with a large, curved claw on its retractable second toe.

tyrannosaurid A member of a group of large carnivorous theropod dinosaurs.

Index